MW00615379

Disasterology

Disasterology

poems

by

Maggie Smith

Dream Horse Press
Aptos, California

Dream Horse Press
Post Office Box 2080
Aptos, California 95001-2080

Printed in the United States of America
Published in 2015 by Dream Horse Press

ISBN 978-1-935716-38-9

Cover artwork:

Dead Air
by painter, Michael Paul Miller

www.mpmart.net

Contents

for Jason

1

I guess you'd currently call it a disaster movie....
End of the world was an earlier genre.
—Michael O'Donoghue

When Worlds Collide (1951)

I think all you scientists are crackpots! Nothing is going to happen.

If Dr. Bronson's calculations prove to be correct,
this will be the most frightening discovery of all time.
The astronomer is convinced a star umpteen times
the size of the sun is barreling straight at us, but
no one believes. His daughter—nicknamed *Stargazer*,
tiny-waisted in tailored suits and pearls—is terrified.
Looking out a taxicab window, she wishes she were
ignorant like all the others, still rushing to work, saving
for a time-share at the beach, planning for the future.
She doesn't want to know the day and time of the end
of the world, or that the only thing to do is hurry up
and build a rocketship, a modern ark bound for a planet
that may not even be habitable. It's a world war
mentality, except they're rationing time. The daughter
knows this, like she knows only forty can be saved
and she's one of them. When the star bears down,
big and orange as a harvest moon, the tin rocketship
lifts off. Her eyes are wild. The pilot she's sweet on
wonders aloud if they'll have enough gas to get there.
It's hard to say—the needle bounces on the fuel gauge,
likely stolen from a '48 Lincoln Continental. It's so
American, coasting in to the new world on fumes.

The Day the Earth Stood Still (1951)

I came here to warn you that by threatening danger, your planet faces danger.

When a Frisbee of strobing light lands on the Mall,
it's to a vibraphone soundtrack. Call headquarters.
Get the Lieutenant. Alert the *extra-extra, read-all-about-it kid.*
Conveniently, the spaceman speaks English, picked up
from American radio—*The Lone Ranger, Little Orphan Annie.*
Soon enough he's on the lam. Because he looks like a banker,
he can go wherever he wants. The boardinghouse beauty
who rents the room next door is either playing rummy
or out with the slick insurance salesman, so the spaceman
takes her cowlicked, *gee mister* boy to see his father
in Arlington National Cemetery. Looking out at row
after row of white tablets, he can't believe all those people
died in wars. Where he lives, the blue Earth looks still,
but up close it's chaos. He doesn't want to believe violence
is all the violent understand. He's out of patience. Finally
the beauty sees: He stills the world to show it can be still.

Invasion of the Body Snatchers (1956)

Only when we have to fight to stay human do we realize how precious it is to us, how dear.

Everything looks the same, but isn't. The blonde is
convinced that the old man mowing the lawn, smoking
his pipe, is not her uncle. Jimmy Grimaldi swears
his mother is not his mother. There's no difference
you can actually see, they say, but something's missing.
The doctor thinks it's a contagious neurosis until
they find a corpse with a vague face, as if unfinished.
*It's like the first impression that's stamped on a coin....
waiting for the final finished face to be stamped onto it.* Soon
he sees his girl's doppelganger in the cellar, gelling
like a fetus. Then a man-sized seed pod foaming,
popping open to reveal his sudsy double. If the doctor
drifts off to sleep, his mind will be absorbed. He can't
even call the police—they're not the police anymore.
They're all in on it, the people he's known all his life.
Now only the sane seem crazy. They're choking down
uppers, chain smoking, fighting to keep their eyes open
all night or else be changed. To escape, they must walk
among imposters. This is what you do to seem reborn:
give nothing away, keep your eyes wide and blank.

On the Beach (1959)

You should have grabbed me, you know. I'm about to be extinct.

America is gone. When Gregory Peck's submarine
reaches San Francisco Bay—*up periscope*—no one's
on Market Street; no cars cross the Bay Bridge.
The Morse Code he's been receiving is just wind
tapping a Coke bottle against the machine. The Cold
War's never been hotter. It's a dystopian future, except
the future is 1964, Fred Astaire helps build the bomb,
and Ava Gardner just wants to smoke and drink
until doomsday. And why not? We're all going to die
someday, except that someday is any minute now,
when the fallout drifts over Australia and everything
is irradiated. Might as well put on a bikini and head
for the beach. Might as well light up another cigarette,
pour yourself another brandy, sing *Waltzing Matilda*
loud and long with the barroom boys—*"You'll never
take me alive," said he.* What are you saving yourself for?
Go ahead, sleep with the submarine captain. Forget
his wife and kids, dead in Connecticut. Go ahead,
forget. Lie back on the sand and soak up the rays.

The Day After (1983)

*You think we're gonna sweep up the dead and fill in a couple of holes
and build some supermarkets?*

When the mushroom cloud rises like a beehive hairdo
over Kansas City, the doctor remembers something
his daughter said about a painting: there's no perspective
because the artist wants you to be part of the landscape.
And he is part of it, seeing white horses incinerated mid-run.
A Missouri plate lies in the rubble—the *Show-Me State*.
But the kids want to take in the light, to lie down
and make angels in the fallout. It's like being inside
a snow globe with tiny barns and a miniature missile silo
that blasts whenever you shake it. Inside the farmhouses,
every television is dialed to static. One man tells his wife
to stop making the beds—who cares if the beds
are a mess! Everyone asks the doctor what he saw,
if anything's left out there, if what seared a child's eyes
is still cooking. If you wind up the globe and shake it,
music plays and a tide of fire drags everything away.

Night of the Comet (1984)

Hey, I'm sorry if the end of the world makes me a little nervous!

Nothing good can come of a comet vaporizing
everyone on Earth except two Valley girls, a trucker,
and scientists holed up in some underground think tank
in the desert. In the empty city, nothing but dust inside
piles of bomber jackets, legwarmers, dresses with wide,
patent-leather belts. As if everyone laid out their clothes
for the next day, then disappeared. But even when a girl
picks up a Reebok and pours out the powdered remains
of a foot, she doesn't cry. She's already begun to forget
their faces, to ignore all the things that don't make sense—
mirrored skyscrapers still reflecting off Wilshire, traffic
lights that still work, the Top 40 station still broadcasting
New Wave, heavy on the keyboards. The girls just want
to have fun. They feather their hair and loot the mall
for designer jeans and sunglasses. The end isn't so bad
after all. Now they can have the whole world for free.

The Quiet Earth (1985)

One: There has been a malfunction with Project Flashlight with devastating results.

Two: It seems I am the only person left on Earth.

When you wake up wearing nothing but a laminated
ID card on a chain around your neck, it's like an acid
flashback: the sun rises over the ocean and the water
simmers. You can dial the lab on your rotary phone,
but all your coworkers are dead. You can drive
the empty streets, walk through the burning shell
of an airplane—the seats all empty, the seatbelts still
neatly buckled. You can read the sign in the garden
store window: *Plant now and grow for the future.* You can
scream all you want, play saxophone in the pouring
rain downtown. Then it hits you: If you are alone,
you can move up in the world. You can find yourself
a manor with a marble staircase and oil paintings
in heavy gold frames. You can have silver tea service,
a silk smoking jacket, a life-sized model auk with real
emu feathers. It's the Make a Wish Foundation
for the last man on Earth. You can drape yourself
in Egyptian cotton sheets and address your subjects
from the balcony like Caesar. They're cardboard
cutouts—the Queen, Hitler, Nixon—but if you slip
a cassette into the deck and press play, a crowd roars.

Armageddon (1998)

It happened before. It will happen again. It's just a question of when.

Houston, the red phone is ringing. Houston, the problem
is the Gulf War ended in '91, but when recliner-sized
asteroids start falling on New York City, a cabbie swears
Saddam is bombing us. Somehow it seems appropriate
that the big one's the size of Texas and nothing can
survive it, not even bacteria. Houston, how can our best
bet be an oil rigger and a nuclear warhead? It's junk
science. Houston, the computer graphics look like Atari
and America looks like the fifties. Kids build shuttles
out of bicycles, cardboard, and tinfoil, and pilot them
in the street. Houston, they're going into tornado cellars,
as if the wooden door and walls of cool dirt will save them.
Everyone on Earth is going underground to show how alike
we really are. Houston, I'd like to buy the world a Coke.
I'd like to believe life's a ride with windmills and dolls
singing in their wooden shoes. Houston, what we have
in common is fear. The red phone is still ringing.
The problem is, Houston, it's a small world after all.

Time of the Wolf (2003)

Everything'll work out. Maybe tomorrow even.....And our mouths will water with roast pigeons, and maybe the dead will come back to life.

Children, you've buried your father in the French
countryside, your mother still has a smear of his blood
on her cheek, evening is becoming more concentrated,
as if someone boiled the water out of it, and you're knocking
on every door, but no one answers. So many lit windows,
but no one will help you. The trains won't stop, no matter
how many times you cry *s'il vous plait*, running alongside.
Find a barn, hold your yellow bird close, sleep. My pets,
it's still a green world out there. If you're cold, peel the coat
off the dead man in the pasture, surrounded by his flock
of dead sheep. Children, when night falls again, reduced
to its black bitters, keep a fire burning. If your mother
wanders, hold up hay torches and call to her. Everything
will be all right. Don't believe the circus man who chews
on razor blades; it's just a trick. It must be hard to tell,
when so many impossible things have been real. My little
treasures, perhaps it's all a trick, a beautiful woman sawed
in half. At the end, the illusionist will bring it all back:
your father, the bird, the shepherd, the sheep. Children,
it will be like any magic show. If you don't believe,
raise your hand. You can walk right up and touch them.

The Road (2009), Which I Can't Finish Watching

I told the boy when you dream about bad things happening, it means you're still fighting and you're still alive. It's when you start to dream about good things that you should start to worry.

A man and his son, alone in the ruined world, two bullets
in the rusted revolver just in case it comes to that.
Nothing but roasted crickets for supper, the chirping
lost in the fire someplace. Where does it go?
The whole map of the world is burned to the edges.
If this were my life, could I teach my daughter
to put the gun to the roof of her mouth? Motherhood
has flipped a switch in me. Even though this isn't real,
even though what I'm seeing isn't nuclear winter
but Pennsylvania, the same deathtrap Breezewood
Turnpike tunnels I drove the year I lived in Gettysburg
and swore I'd never drive again, I have to turn it off.
While the man and his boy have shelter and real food:
Cheetos, Del Monte fruit in light syrup, Vitamin Water.
While they have warm, dry bunks and something
approximating hope, but it can't be hope. The music
tells us it's safe, but it won't last. There's an hour left,
and it can't be all candlelight and canned peaches.

2

Never think you've seen the last of anything.
—Eudora Welty

Last Night on Earth

I play Last Night on Earth by closing my eyes
and convincing myself it will all be gone

when I open them: streets lined with pear trees;
crosswalks and people crossing. Waiting
in darkness, I am Pennsylvania dawn before

the sun steamrolls the hills with its flattening
wave of light, before the mist rises off the cows'

shoulders. I am the mist. No, I'm grass so tall,
a child could wade in and never come out.
I am the dime-sized lights blinking at twilight,

calling him inside. No, I am the reedy
imprints on the boy's legs when they find him.
I am the phone ringing in his mother's house

and what is said, the reply to which
is a strangling sound. No, I'm his birthstone

in a pendant she wore, believing it
kept him safe. I am the space inside her
once occupied by that belief. I am the remainder

after loss is equated, the little R beside the zero.
In darkness, I am everything one last time.

No, I am their absence. I am a shrine
to lost streets, trees, crosswalks, crossers.
Oh, I wish the pear trees could stay—

just the pear trees. But if everything is gone,
what could I possibly offer to save them?

Last Night on Earth always ends this way.
Winning means I can't bear to look,
sure the world has dissolved

around me, wondering if I've been spared
because the nothing demands to be seen.

Green

Fact: The threat level has never been lowered nationwide to Blue or Green.

By the time it was named, Green had gone the way
of dinosaurs and New Coke. Now the New York
afternoons are Orange. Evenings, too.
Not creamsicle, but car flare. Everywhere else
is Yellow, which could be cheerful if it weren't
so constantly elevated. If it weren't piped like
Musak into every crevice. Today is a new day.
I've never seen it before, so it must qualify
as out of the ordinary. Maybe I should report it
to the authorities. In these perilous times,
I am vigilant. I take notice of my surroundings.
I am aware of each morning's insurgence
of sunlight. At the real end of the unreal
world, if you see something, say something.
Green, had I known, I would have memorized
every last detail. I would have alerted everyone.

Fimbulwinter

What the ice gets, the ice keeps.

—Ernest Shackleford

At first the frost is like a second skin,
all silvery. It makes you look like magic,

your skyline like a row of wedding cakes—
domes, arches, spires frosted white.

Oh my city, my icebox full of sweets.
Everywhere, ice sculptures are hailing

taxi cabs, walking their dogs. Thick
ribbons of birds are fleeing. Oh my city,

the little bergs on your river interlock
like puzzle pieces. I could walk on water

from here to the edge of the earth if there
were anything left. But I won't leave you.

I won't stand on a rooftop, waving my arms,
striking the last spent match over and over.

No one's coming. No one's getting out.
Even the birds freeze into paperweights,

fall, and shatter. Oh my city, you're still
and dark at the end. But when the moon

dangles overhead like a mirror ball,
every inch of you sparkles and writhes.

Orientation

Because you're new here, you need someone,
but I'm too busy trying to keep you
in the twentieth century a while longer,
feeding logs into the woodstove's glowing mouth
while, in a house just down the street,
someone programs a thermostat.
Twentieth century? Who am I kidding?
It was never safe. In this young country,
you can trace danger farther than you can
follow it, back to fire licking the walls of caves,
back to flint skinning the animal to its source.
Nothing predates danger. A hundred years ago,
Roosevelt Avenue was not this green
tunnel of London planes, only rows of saplings
planted by someone looking toward the future
where we now live, always looking forward
or back. The twentieth century didn't
keep me, but not for lack of trying.
I made it out alive. What can I say but stay
alive? You're new, and there's too much to learn.

Future

What is the future?

Everything that hasn't happened yet, the future
is tomorrow and next year and when you're old
but also in a minute or two, when I'm through
answering. The future is nothing I imagined
as a child: no jet packs, no conveyor-belt sidewalks,
no bell-jarred cities at the bottom of the sea.
The trick of the future is that it's empty,
a cup before you pour the water. The future
is a waiting cup, and for all it knows, you'll fill it
with milk instead. You're thirsty. Every minute
carries you forward, conveys you, into a space
you fill. I mean the future will be full of you.
It's one step beyond the step you're taking now.
It's what you'll say next until you say it.

The Disasterologist

She's beginning to think her life's work
has been for nothing. What conference
can she attend with the paper *Everything's Bad*

and Only Getting Worse? What happened
to *Time Heals All Wounds* or *We're Never Given
More than We Can Handle?* They died

in notecard stage. The disasterologist's job
is to prove what no one wants proved:
Bad things don't happen in threes.

They keep coming down the conveyor belt
like Lucy and Ethel's chocolates
and no one can keep up. She knows

her work is done. Disaster is capable
of proving itself. It will outlast us,
a greyhound chasing a mechanical

rabbit until it runs itself to death,
but in reverse: Disaster is the machine
chasing the living thing.

The New Regime Is Making Itself Right at Home

in the hand-me-down clothes of the old regime,
which fit perfectly. It's commandeered the record
collection, strewed them all across the bedroom floor.
It refuses to slip them back into their paper jackets.
It turns up the volume and won't answer the phone.
You know what to do at the beep. The new regime's
wearing its hair in the old regime's style. It's using
shampoo and conditioner left in the shower.
It's driving the car around the city, in dark glasses.
It dabs the old regime's perfume on its pulse points.
In bed, the old regime's boyfriend can't even tell
the difference. The new regime pastes its face
over the old's in the yearbook. It inherits all
the same superlatives, laughs at the same jokes.
The new regime's here to stay. It's eating off
the family china, watching the TV. It's looking out
the old regime's window, and the view is the same.

Big Bang

How did the world get here?

Space broke like a black plate into pieces,
and one piece is the world. The rest are floating,
the contents of a suitcase unzipped in zero gravity.
No, it won't happen again. There is no space
explosion drill, no county siren keening
and pushing us underground. The Big Bang
can't happen again because it's still happening:
we are mid-explosion as we drive to the closest
and worst post office in town, the one
with the longest line, the postage machine
always out-of-order. Our letter stamped *forever*
flies to someone who isn't. The universe is still
expanding but so slowly we don't notice the pieces
of not-world pulling away from the world.

Eliza

There are more stars in the sky than sounds
uttered by all people who have ever lived,

but Eliza, we may never see them again.
Down in the cellar with the preserves,

away from danger, you wipe clean the dusty
jars and hold them to whatever light

you can muster. Even here the fruit
glows like a fiery jewel, but neither color

nor sweetness can sustain us. Child, we can't
know what's left. Maybe we're alone

or maybe other cellars on this street
fill with whispers. Underground the air

is still. You're like a bottled ship, no wind
to fill your sails. I know you want to crack

the door, Eliza, to see if any stars
remain, threading their light through tiny holes

in nail-pierced tin. I want to show the moon
to you, busted hunk of concrete, seashell

pieces broken up inside it—fossils
left over from the world before us. Maybe

our bones will whiten it next, but for now
the moon is just a story I tell. Trust me,

child, the moon is not like this. It lives
high where the air is sweet to breathe. The moon

holds itself up to its own light. The moon
is up—the opposite of all you know.

Twentieth Century

I must have missed the last train out of this gray city.
I'm scrolling the radio through *shhhhh*. The streetlamps

fill with light, right on time, but no one is pouring it in.
Twentieth Century, you're gone. You're tucked into

a sleeping car, rolling to god-knows-where, and I'm
lonely for you. I know it's naïve. But your horrors

were far away, and I thought I could stand them.
Twentieth Century, we had a good life more or less,

didn't we? You made me. You wove the long braid
down my back. You kissed me in the snowy street

with everyone watching. You opened your mouth a little
and it scared me. Twentieth Century, it's *me*, it's *me*.

You said that to me once, as if I'd forgotten your face.
You strung me out until trees seemed to breathe,

expanding and contracting. You played "American Girl"
and turned it up loud. You said I was untouchable.

Do you remember the nights at Alum Creek, the lit
windows painting yellow Rothkos on the water?

Are they still there, or did you take them with you?
Say something. I'm here, waiting, scrolling the radio.

On every frequency, someone hushes me. Is it you?
Twentieth Century, are you there? I thought you were

a simpler time. I thought we'd live on a mountain
together, drinking melted snow, carving hawk totems

from downed pines. We'd never come back. Twentieth
Century, I was in so deep, I couldn't see an end to you.

Acknowledgments

Thanks to the editors of the following journals, in which certain of these poems first appeared, sometimes in slightly different versions or with different titles:

Alaska Quarterly Review: "Fimbulwinter" & "Twentieth Century"
Carbon Copy Magazine: "Invasion of the Body Snatchers (1956)" & "The Quiet Earth (1985)"
diode: "Future," "The New Regime" & "Orientation"
Hayden's Ferry Review: "The Disasterologist"
Jabberwock Review: "Eliza"
The Journal: "Armageddon (1998)"
New Ohio Review: "On the Beach (1959)"
Third Coast: "Last Night on Earth"
West Branch: "The Day the Earth Stood Still (1951)," "Night of the Comet (1984)," "Time of the Wolf (2003)" & "When Worlds Collide (1951)"

"When Worlds Collide (1951)" was reprinted by *Verse Daily*. "The Day the Earth Stood Still (1951)," "Night of the Comet (1984)," "The Quiet Earth (1985)," "When Worlds Collide (1951)," and "Eliza" were reprinted in the anthology *Apocalypse Now: Poems and Prose from the End of Days*, edited by Andrew McFadyen-Ketchum and Alexander Lumans (Upper Rubber Boot Books, 2012). "Green" was printed in the anthology *What Happened to Us These Last Couple Years?* edited by David Barringer (Elope Press/So New Publishing, 2008).

Thanks to the National Endowment for the Arts, the Ohio Arts Council, and the Virginia Center for the Creative Arts for fellowships that made this work possible. Special thanks to Katie Pierce, my first and best reader, and to my husband, Jason Beehler, who watched the world end (or narrowly escape destruction) over and over again with me.

CPSIA information can be obtained
at www.ICGtesting.com
Printed in the USA
BVHW072103210122
626772BV00008B/1031

9 781935 716389